Advice from the Lights

Also by Stephen Burt

Poetry

Belmont
Parallel Play
Popular Music
All-Season Stephanie (chapbook)
Why I Am Not a Toddler by Cooper Bennett Burt (chapbook)

Nonfiction

The Poem Is You: 60 Contemporary American Poems and How to Read Them
The Art of the Sonnet
Close Calls with Nonsense: Reading New Poetry
The Forms of Youth: Twentieth-Century Poetry and Adolescence
Randall Jarrell and His Age

Advice from the Lights

Poems

STEPHEN BURT

Graywolf Press

This publication is made possible, in part, by the voters of Minnesota through a Minnesota State Arts Board Operating Support grant, thanks to a legislative appropriation from the arts and cultural heritage fund, and a grant from the Wells Fargo Foundation. Significant support has also been provided by Target, the McKnight Foundation, the Lannan Foundation, the Amazon Literary Partnership, and other generous contributions from foundations, corporations, and individuals. To these organizations and individuals we offer our heartfelt thanks.

Published by Graywolf Press
250 Third Avenue North, Suite 600
Minneapolis, Minnesota 55401

www.graywolfpress.org

Published in the United States of America

ISBN 978-1-55597-789-4

2 4 6 8 9 7 5 3 1
First Graywolf Printing, 2017

Library of Congress Control Number: 2017930116

Cover design: Kapo Ng

Cover art: Shutterstock

to Cooper and Nathan and Jessie
for our present and our future

Contents

5

"I grew up in the human world," September said crossly.

"It's not the same," Hawthorn sighed. "You don't know what it's like to always, always feel that you don't belong, to your family, to your city, or your school, knowing there's something different about you, something off, that you're not like the others, that you're an alien all alone."

September crossed her arms. "Hawthorn. *Everyone* feels like that."   —Catherynne M. Valente,
The Girl Who Raced Fairyland All the Way Home

I felt entirely connected to the time and place in which I was writing the songs, and so believed that those around me would feel the same as me and would understand them.

—Tracey Thorn, *Bedsit Disco Queen*

She would not say of anyone in the world now that they were this or were that. She felt very young; at the same time unspeakably aged.   —Virginia Woolf, *Mrs. Dalloway*

Nothing is everything to everyone. That is, compromises will have to be made.   —Bryan Walpert, *Native Bird*

Ice for the Ice Trade

Everybody wants a piece of me.

I have been weighed and measured,
tested and standardized,
throughout my young life. It happens to everyone,
or to everyone with my ability.

Now I live quietly
and mostly in the dark, amid sawdust and sheer
or streaky wooden surfaces. My role,
when I reach maturity,
may be to help people behave
more sociably, and reduce
the irritations of summer,
or else to make it easier to eat.

For reasons I cannot fathom, I weep when it rains.
My handlers keep me wrapped in awkward cloth.
They will not let me touch my friends
or show any curves. They have taught me how to shave.

A few twigs and dragonfly wings got caught
near the center of me long ago; they serve
to distinguish me from others of my kind,
along with some bubbles of air.

I am worth more when I am clear.
When I am most desirable
you should be able to see yourself through me.

Some of my distant relatives
will probably never go far,
because they are too irregular, or opaque.
Many of us will end on a cart.

I, on the other hand, have had my work
cut out for me by so many gloves
and tongs, pallets and barges, poles and planks
that I am sure I will go to New York;
there people who own
the rights to me will give elaborate thanks
to one another, and go on to take me apart.

My 1979

I was Mr. Spock being raised by Dr. Spock.
I was told I was free,
but only free to be me.
I knew I loved my digital clock.

I would have trusted my instincts if I had any,
or if I could have given them a name.
I was deceived by the body that I mistook for a bad penny,
by the shimmery beauty of my immediate peers,
which I mistook for fame.

By wearing them over and over without socks
I let my one pair of gold tennis shoes fall apart.
I regarded the temporary reassembly of the Styrofoam packing parts
that came with small household appliances as a fine art.
Inhabited by C-3POs, they became
starbases, or soft-focus all-white homes of the future.
I wanted to think that they had nothing to fear.
I ate peanut butter and pimento sandwiches every day for at least a week,
at most, for half a year.

I had become convinced
that character was fate.
Almost anything could result in tears.
I wanted to stay at Alison's house overnight
and wake up as a new girl, or a new mutant,
or a new kind of humanity, engineered
to travel at more than half the speed of light,
but I wasn't allowed. My bedtime and I were both eight.

Hermit Crab

That shell is pretty, but that shell is too small for me.

Each home is a hideout; each home is a secret; each home
is a getaway under the same hot lamp, a means
to a lateral move at low velocity.

I live in a room in the room
of a boy I barely see.

Sometimes the boy and his talkative friends raise
too-warm hands and try to set me free

and I retreat into myself, hoping they place
me back in my terrarium, and they
do, with disappointed alacrity.

Scatter patterns in sand, adnates, cancellates, gaping
whelk husks, a toy tractor-trailer, cracked
and dinged, beside the spine of a plastic tree,

the helmet-shaped shelter of a shadow cast
by a not-quite-buried wedge of pottery . . .

if I have a body that's wholly my own
then it isn't mine. For a while I was
protected by what I pretended to be.

Princess Stephanie

To be delicate, to be too big for the helpless, too little and too important

To have to say: help me out of this tulle dress

I know how to kiss but not how to do this slow dance

What use is the adult world? It doesn't have unicorns

Why can't I wear two different colored shoes?

A Covered Bridge in Littleton, New Hampshire

I can remember when I wanted X
more than anything ever—for X fill in
from your own childhood

[balloon, pencil lead, trading card, shoelaces, a bow
or not to have to wear a bow]

and now I am moved to action, when I am moved,
principally by a memory of what to want.

The point is to be, in your own eyes, what you are,

or to keep your own tools, so that you can pretend.

And so it was no surprise,
to me at least, when Cooper, who is two,
collapsed in *fortissimo* fits when he could not have
a $20, three-foot-long stuffed frog
in the image of Frog from *Frog and Toad*, since he is Toad.

That morning, needing a nap,
he had thrown, from the third-story balcony
of Miller's Cafe and Bakery, into the whistling
rapids and shallows
of the Ammonoosuc River, with its arrowheads and caravans of stones,
his Red Sox cap. His hair was shining like
another planet's second sun,
as he explained, looking up, "I threw my hat in the river.
I would like my hat back now."

My 1980

It was now my younger brothers who had
philosophical objections to taking a bath.

After I came back from the optician,
gold backs for earrings, aglets and fish scales,

erasers' edges, girls' clean fingernails,
were no longer fuzzy, a probability cloud,

but evident in separate outlines, sad
as Atari pixels with their 8-bit math.

I had not the means but the active imagination—
so adults said—to go anywhere: for example,

into the Earth's hot mantle
in a box-elder-bug-shaped burrowing ironclad.

I was the stowaway on an Edwardian liner
who knew what the locket's ancient pictographs meant,

thanks to my prior study of Egyptology,
delighting the princess by proving she was not cursed.

I was also the unaccompanied minor
afraid to look down, or out at the Atlantic,

as we began our rickety descent
toward Fort Lauderdale-Hollywood International Airport.

I thought of myself as omniscient, as ichthyomantic.
I wanted to spend the following week immersed

in sea-floor adventures, a Nebula-winning tetralogy,
or swimming, as a kind of last resort.

Over Sacramento

The sky is platinum blonde,
so bright I avert my eyes.
Everything is a staple, a fret, an acre of salt, some twine
laid flat on sand with nothing caught inside.

One part of bad news,
psychological researchers say, cancels five parts of good;

one line of will and must, of take what you get,
can cancel out a line of wish or would.

Please, everybody alive,
do your best to stay that way.
It's hard enough to grieve for talented strangers,
albeit they did not seem so. There will be no more songs

brought down to this Earth by Scott Miller of Sacramento
and Davis, CA: the author, while there,
of "Bad Year at UCLA,"
and later of "Don't Bother Me While I'm Living Forever,"
of "Song About 'Rocks Off'"—but not, of course, of "Rocks Off"—

of "I've Tried Subtlety," the least subtle
among his disgruntled effects, and of "Aerodeliria,"
which begins *Aerodeliria jet ride, it don't affect me now*
and whose chorus concludes *I don't think we'll ever lose*—no more misdirections,

intuitive puns or unfolded misconceptions,
no more mathematical games
or matrices made up of names,
nothing to graph or get lost in,
nothing else for needy, supposedly
gifted children to put that level of trust in

as of today
(and the blocky clouds fold up
as if hiding behind themselves in a rolling moiré)
who left us not so much,
or rather not only, with so many finished songs
as with the sense that he had more to say.

Kites

Complete in ourselves,
we look like scraps of paper anyway:
        left alone, we could tell

our mothers and one another our owners'
        flimsiest secrets and play together all day

        until we became intertwined, which is why
you try
        to keep us permanently apart.

One of us is a gossamer pirate ship,
        a frigate whose rigging the industrial

        sunset highlights, sail by oblong sail.
Another resembles a Greek letter—gamma,
        or lambda; others still

a ligature, a propeller, a fat lip.
        Our will is not exactly the wind's will.
Underlined by sand,

        whose modes of coagulation and cohabitation
none of the human pedestrians understand,

we take off on our almost arbitrarily
        lengthy singletons of string

        toward the unattainable, scarily
lofty realm of hawk and albatross
        and stay, backlit by cirrocumulus.

        It seems to be up to you
to keep us
        up in the air, and to make sure our paths never cross.

Swans at a Pond by JFK Airport

resemble cranes,
the construction kind; one of the pair has begun to assemble

a nest as big
as a sleeping adult human being. No rest

accrues to the
weary, if the weary are or expect to be parents; but no blues,

no keening, no
jeremiads are in order, just advice they won't hear: *take it slow;*

try, at least, to
make plans you won't have to keep: you, too, will cry.

Futurity
appears here as several bits of mess: split sticks, dull loot

our trenches leave,
prismatic drinking straws, and bottlenecks belie the merely emotional power

source that some of
us find in recycling, as if we could rescue a watershed by collating apple cores,

as if goodness
were easy to recognize, and the way to tell *eros* from *caritas*

elementary.
O swans, mute, self-appointed landed gentry

whose work confines
itself to the under-studied and overlooked, further reports would only confuse

us who travel
in such exhausting, overbearing vehicles, and make ourselves ridiculous

thereby. It is
not we who own the air.

To the Naked Mole Rats at the National Zoo

Bucktoothed and semitransparent, pretty to no one,
butt of a joke and protagonist of a cartoon,
you make ridicule
seem inescapable,
not at home anywhere
sunlight might penetrate the circuitous air,
or else at home only on paper,
a mockup of a colony on the moon.
What with the light fixtures' shadows and the (exhale, inhale, exhale)
    water vapor,
your tunnels look almost opaque,
their entrance strobing like a zoetrope:
some unambitious version of heaven,
or mild first level of hell. Alexander Pope,
with his grotto and chronic pain, might have had a lot
to say about your lot,
so eager to immure
one another, yet always on view
to the grade schoolers whose eyes, below woven
caps and sun hats, make a meal of you.
They could see you as unfinished, or as a mistake.
One compared you to severed toes.
Another called all of you "skin tubes," which seems apropos,
if rude; it describes us all, though your motives are pure,
your will therefore harder to break.

My 1981

Everyone's younger sibling was still in a stroller,
learning to drink from a cup or stay in a dress.
Everyone's mom was overseeing additions

to our beige, orange, and air-conditioned kitchens,
choosing the tiles: cake batter, peach, mallow, rose-pink.
They matched the crayons that matched our skins.

Everyone's dad was a lawyer, or else in government service.
Our teachers were also moms. They returned our work
on time, with stars, in green and purple ink.

I had one friend who was actually my friend:
he liked to argue that law-abiding Americans
would end up safer if we all owned guns.

He knew about BMXes, and how to surf,
or said he did. I didn't know what to think.
Each week on TV we awaited the motorcycles

of the bold, law-abiding, wisecracking police.
All summer his little sister ran circles around us
so we decided she had to be the Flash.

After his friends' older friends
TP'd the split-level houses
beside our own, rain turned their thinning banners
the color of sunburnt, crumpled American cash.

Inside Outside Stephanie

1

I made myself. Mommy and Daddy were proud, in that order.
I didn't mail myself like a letter some other kids
already knew. I learned to use stamps. They stuck to my thumb
without any glue. I didn't have any permission.

2

There was a snowstorm that lasted three days
and a cavern of monochrome memory. There were board games, and a
    pencil-and-paper game
where the object was to figure out the object of the game.
There was a stack of broad-rule writing paper, and a stapled calendar,
and a 64-pack of sparkly rainbow crayons, to make each week look different
since they all started out black and white, and all the same.

3

O grapefruit (as color and flavor). O never quite rightly tied laces. O look,
up there on the uneven climbing bars,
too hot to touch where the sun touches, now that it's spring,

the shadow of a tarp, like a sail between sailors
and thin swings that make no decision, like weather vanes.

O think of the lost Chuck Taylors. The lost Mary Janes.

Scarlet, a Betta

for Amanda Schaffer

I'm really bright blue. I keep going back and forth
between trying to live up to my name
and following my reflection, or my nature.

I know no east, no north,
no consequence, or permanence, or blame;
I regard the curious child
who feeds me as a disinterested creator,
neither beloved nor reviled.

I reserve my love
for holy Ariel,
my admiration for the king of the sea,
inch-high, great-bearded Neptune, whose silent rule
extends over bubbles, and artificial
coral, and a filtration system, and me.

All the colors I recognize are alive
in the pebbles at the bottom of my tank.
I pretend each trace or trail
I make in the clarified water
amounts to my emphatic signature,
which I have chosen to leave in invisible ink.

Roly-Poly Bug

Non serviam

Because I can't ever appear
as I would like to appear,
I once tried to make it so you couldn't see me at all.

I named myself after a pill
but it didn't help. I liked
the feeling of feeling small,

as long as it let me feel mobile; I wanted to roll
up and down and around the tiny hall

of a groove in discarded cardboard. I used to appall
my peers with risky behavior. I might fall

to my death in a half-inch ditch
full of oil or lawnmower grease. I stall

at the brush of a fingertip. I'm so afraid
of a grand faux pas that I answer the most banal

questions by quoting the questioner, so as to let
his words shield mine. I cover my anger
imperfectly, so I can breathe

with my head between my ten legs; I am my own
backyard slat fence, my own slate garden wall.

I am chitin and ichor inside, but I'll never let on
how I look underneath. I could always make something
else of myself. I could be having a ball.

After Callimachus

So reactionaries and radicals complain
          that I have no proprietary mission,
no project that's all mine;
          instead, I am like a child flipping Pogs
or building with Minecraft bricks, although I'm past forty.
          To them I say: keep rolling logs
for one another, but don't waste my time
          imposing your inappropriate ambition:
marathon runners and shock jocks gain
          by going as far as they can, but the sublime,
the useful, and the beautiful in poetry
          are all inversely correlated
with size: shorter means sweeter. I'll be fine.
                    When I first rated
myself as a writer of some sort,
          wolf-killing, light-bearing Apollo came to me
as a ferret. Stay off crowded trains, he said; never resort
          to volume where contrast will do. Imitate
Erik Satie, or Young Marble Giants. The remedy for anomie
          lies in between the wing-slips of the cicada.
If I can't be weightless, or glide among twigs, or sate
          myself on dew, then let
                    my verses live that way,
since I feel mired in age, and worse for wear.
          It might even be that when the Muses visit
a girl, or a schoolboy, they intend to stay,
          or else to come back, even after the poet goes gray.

Palinode with Playmobil Figurines

They do not move. They cannot bend their knees.
When we go to bed, the Redcoats do not sit down
to a cold Sunday joint and an eighteenth-century
discussion of natural moralities.
Nor can they constitute corporations, or sail
away from us all in a catamaran
beyond the range of the ceiling fan. Their band
has never disassembled its microphone stand
in order to build a tower for 2 Hz
radio signals whose primes summon alien beings.
Their girls cannot link hands;
their smooth-faced construction workers in orange jumpsuits
with decals for zippers, their knights of suzerain lands
in smoothly painted-on armor, cannot insist
on byrnies or jazerants that nobody sees.
They do not move. They cannot bend their knees.

Their niece, with her persimmon bowl cut, never flees
her own maple-strewn backyard; she will never steal
the breeches from a stranger's line, nor find
camaraderie and peril upon the high seas.
Nor does the glossy-eyed butterfly princess pose,
still sullen, before her regent; she will never hold
her crown shakily in round fingers—more bronze than gold,
more circlet or torc than crown—nor attempt to postpone
her marriage to her scrofulous second cousin
despite their mothers' frenetic diplomacies;
her bearded, big-eyed uncle never removes
his wig, and never disagrees.
All of them know how to read. None fears the tale
of the monkey's paw, how by wishing to make
your family perfect you kill it; none of them have
to cease, or pause, their play while another one pees.

None of them know how low
the imagination recedes,
how you end up doing only what other
people remind you to do,
thus fashioning the new life to which
a responsible person cedes
in some sort of ecstatic resignation
in the same way that kids learn when to say please.
Given their hollow heads, their sturdy
cylindrical necks, they could almost know how to breathe,
though none of them breathes. They cannot bend their knees.

My 1982

I had a future in the dark.
At Putt-Putt Mini Golf, Arcade and Recreation Park,
I stood up and twitched as if in labs' fume hoods,
divorced, like other seventh-graders' parents,
both from evil and from good.

I had to stop to pee, pull up my pants,
or unpick grit from a trackball.
Some games relied, like social life, on patterns:
remember each action and its consequence
and you would never get killed, or fail, or fall.
Others demanded adrenalin, norepinephrine,
alertness fit for national defense.

At home, I kept trying and failing to play
piano parts for "Roundabout" and "Long Distance Runaround,"
whose singer's futuristic poise, high A
and strenuous façade of confidence
seemed to mean he belonged to the heavens, where there would be
no difference between the voices of girls and men.

I wanted to sing about c, about optimization,
about hypergolic propellants and hydrazine,
the histories of rocketry and electricity
from amber to Goddard by way of Leyden jars.
My panoply of inappropriate postures
included the extreme slouch and the backward lean,
accomplished out of overcompensation
and a wish to look as if I were watching the stars.

Fifth Grade Time Capsule

Having given the sun and school
    their expected, ceremonious farewells,
I can start to envision my future, my big reveal.

    By that point everything I have kept
between my boards, in my polyurethane seal,
    will have acquired fresh appeal

as evidence from another age:
    a glitter-pen sketch of a tubular rocketship;
an origami-cricket notebook page,

    a jadeite earring, the *Boston Globe*, and a scallop-
necked T-shirt graced with an entourage
    of names in Sharpie, in graffiti script.

I know I am too young to date.
    My answer to everything is "It's too early to say."
Though I am ready to lead a long-delayed

    or even a buried life, I dream of the day
when I am decoded and vaunted, of a floral float in a parade
    if not a chauffeured evening on the town.

The people who pick me up can never be
    the same as the ones who put me down.

Cloud Studies

1

Little vertical stripes—

the ring of nervous children at a dance class,
who cling to the walls on every side of the gym.

Then one line's white, so low on the horizon
above the harbor and above New Haven,

a tape measure on a flat map,

the other tufted, lofty, repeatedly shaped
like "product" in deliberately mussed hair,

and over that, nothing, as if to say, pay it no mind.

2

Massive non-replicability problems. The field
has taken a bad methodological turn

that makes even foundational results unreliable.

One nor'easter after another
                 ice crystals up high
whose sparkle distraction
                 glow
sunset shimmer sublimity
                 logic or lot

has set a bar so high nobody can clear it.

What's up? A place that's way, way overhead.

We will have to reinvent our views
our angles our tint our sense of when you be the judge

before we can look up that way again.

My 1983

When I told Marina I liked her new striped tunic
but there was a hole in her armpit, under her sleeve,

I thought I was making a generous, helpful gesture,
an appropriate social move.

That was the year when we studied the Great Depression,
the business cycle, and macroeconomics.

Companies grew by meeting familiar demands,
or else by spreading news about new pleasures.

I wanted programmable gloves that could make you bionic,
whose workings I laid out in series, in graph-paper pictures;

I diagrammed volts and resistors, tongue-and-groove,
the difference between graphic novels and newspaper comics,

also a parallelogram-based function for love.
I gave a whole series of ten-minute lunchtime lectures

about linguistics to playground structures. "Steve,"
my favorite teacher told me, "you'll probably use

those theories someday and your future colleagues will thank
you for all of them, but we'd like you to think

about what might be interesting to your friends,
not just about what's interesting to you."

Black Raspberry Canes

No more than three deep in the Tupperware bucket; that way
a few handfuls fresh from their twigs would ride
downhill without crushing one another and stay
distinct amid their glossy
tiny reticules, their black-on-black embossed
like ridges on an alligator hide.

The longer I waited the riper they got,
as long as I kept track, as long as I had not
waited too late in the day; then I found dots,
scabs, stems, pale caps or buttons, bird-eaten or parched.

Nobody, my father said, could get so many
scrapes and scratches accidentally:
without them I probably would not have liked it so much.
Here was a part of nature
no one else would want to touch.

The berries came off when pulled gently,
between middle finger and thumb.
The first ones to look ready evidently
had no source of shade, and nothing to come
between their clusters and the close attentions
of the unrelenting sun.

First Kiss Stephanie

Gummi candy, passed back and forth, and slightly stale.

    "But if I *did* like boys—"

Taboos at Twelve

As well as feeling adventurous
I am sad
when I pad
my bra, or my imagined training bra,
because there's no future in it:
there might never be any more there than there is now.
I never asked anybody when to begin it,
but learned about it first by playing "I Never."
However,
I was freed
when I peed
my pants, or panties,
or whatever you call those;
if I could break that rule
then I could break any rule,
so the rules I follow must all be rules I chose.

Esprit Stephanie

The hard work of appearances disappears
into the apparent effortlessness, and the loose three-quarter sleeves

of trying to become what other
people, your friends, your real friends, are convinced that you already are,

like trying to follow the pale fleck of a small plane,
or a big plane far away.

Sweatshirts big enough to hide half a person
hide behind their modular words,

and leggings. Where two or three strangers gather
together, sandbar: we are migratory birds,

temporarily almost aloft, almost fluorescent, in a 1983
of lemon-yellow possibilities,

things I might very insistently wish to be.
Only an eyelash separates me from reason,

from the coveted role of pretty-to-geeky liason.
To be good, to be

a good girl, is to pile up
credit you have to use up

before nobody else remembers you earned it.
There was a lesson in variability here, and in the history

of stencils, but I am not the girl who learned it.
When I got here first I looked around, and around.

I would like to compare my own growing up
to sand, and you and you to solid ground.

After Callimachus

Half of me—an intangible half—is alive;
      the other part has gone I don't know where—
either it's dead, or it's lost in what it calls love.
      Actually it's a flighty tween
delighted by jelly shoes. "Keep your eyes
      on the printed page; stop playing with your hair,"
I tell her, "and put down your portable screen!"
      No use. I'm supposed to profess
        that maturity is a gift,
but I don't believe it, or else I don't care.
      I amble the library stacks and get lost in YA;
I want to go home, paint my nails until they iridesce,
      clamp on my headphones, and pray to Taylor Swift.

The Cars' Greatest Hits

for Timothy Alborn

When everything is artificial, everything
is equally sincere.

I was a ridiculous child,
tall tree made of cloth in my ear.

I got a hold on you, you're all
I've got tonight, you might think I'm delir-

ious, but all I want is you—
How the rankest cliché can please if you can
put yourself where it's what you hoped to hear.

Hexagonal drum pads, Pac-Man tones and tunes
as slick as waterslides
in a summer New England characterized

by who's got a crush on who,
lo-res graphics and kisses on acrylic collars
presented as mysteries to revere—

although *you can't go on*
thinking nothing's wrong is right

enough, if you have the right shades,
if you let somebody else steer.

If you synthesize your confidence, the more
you make up the less you have to fear.

Thank you for making 1984
as good as any other year.

Mean Girls

after Baudelaire

In twos and threes on bedspreads the color of sand
Anywhere in suburban America they turn
Their parallel painted toes to the horizon
Finding a target almost without knowing it hand

On hand together as on a hand-drawn
Ouija board they select
A number to dial a name to call and deflect
The reputation that would land on them

They betray their confidences with confidence
Some of them used to walk through the last wild stand
Of maples behind the cul-de-sac snapping the saplings
Calling each other crybabies they mock experience

And mock my lack of experience
Their net composed of telephone cords
Night after night brings up ghosts
Lantern fish and anglerfish with their intense

Lures are not more fit more deftly set
For such secretive nights such high-pressure atmospheres
Such canticles of devotion to amoral gods
Some of them open the liquor cabinet

In an otherwise empty household and discover
The pleasure of Limoncello and headachy sleep
Some of them mock me for paying
Too much for a sparkly tunic or for looking cheap

They say your black bracelets and grave
Demeanor augur solitary nights
But your slutty hoop earrings must hurt You liked
The right boys but in the wrong order You called it a rave

But it was not a rave You are too good
An accessory kiss-off show-off You disgust
Our modesty You have nothing to show They place air quotes
Around your life so you learn not to trust

Yourself any more than they trust
One another because you still crave
Their pathetic and fleeting attention O monstrous martyrs
With your emerald contact lenses O terrible saints
Of hypocrisy penlites and brave
Cursive in sealed envelopes You understand

How some of us you reject will never forget you
We will grow up to study your mistakes
As means of navigation You wanted to keep
Us from becoming like you but we will not let you

3

My 1985

I wasn't a math star, but one or two of my new friends were.
I liked to work into casual conversation

fusillades of words like *nexus* and *tensor*.
The counselor from the department of recreation

said I had the voice of an angry thirty-year-old.
I thought I had a "penetrating gaze";

kids thought I was staring at them. I had to be told.
After that, I imagined I lived on the moon for two days;

I stood out and hid there, a demented sentry
from an awkwarder parallel world, a young Bizarro.

On our class trip to the beach and the World of Tomorrow,
the boys were igneous. I was sedimentary:

I set out to lie with the other girls on the low dunes
before the morning heat got metamorphic.

They folded their towels and moved off, so I closed my eyes
on the hypothesis that it would make me calmer.

In the talent show, I played piano for Annabelle's show tunes
(we rehearsed extra for passages marked "improvise")

then sang "Take a Pebble" by Emerson Lake & Palmer.
They thought I was caterwauling. I thought I was Orphic.

Fairy Story Stephanie

After I pricked myself
in my ring finger, deliberately, with a pin
because I wanted to feel something in my own body

that I had done on my own, I couldn't
sleep for a week, or not
for more than an hour at a time.
I was the sun in June; I was ready to set,
all amber and solar gel, and me craving the lead.

I want to be found but I wanted to be hard to find.
I have the longest lashes and the least patience,
and if strangers admire my powers I won't mind
having to stand forever, waiting in line.

I stole a shiny cylinder
of cucumber lip gloss from the CVS,

a serpent's tooth from the leaves of our beech tree.
Until recently
I could not tell any difference
between "I want to meet people like me,"
"I want people to like me,"
and "I want to go out of my way to meet people like me

except that I want there to be nobody like me,
only a mirror in air
and a series of shimmery alien sympathies.
Thank you for all the time that you and your friends
let me pay attention to me paying attention to me."

Herring Gull

I always look hungry. I always look the same.
To tell me apart from my brothers you might have to trace
the sunset-orange spot on my beak as I stay in one place,
or tag my heel or say my given name.

In a position of confident wariness
easy to take, or mistake, for weariness,
my head flicks back and forth like a swivel chair
in need of lubrication or minor repair.

I would be graceful, somewhere.
I want to persuade myself that I don't care.
I decline to compete with your kites, which can go far higher,
but cannot change direction on their own.
Nor can they stay—I have seen them flee, or expire—
if their companions leave them alone.

The froth of the whitening surf can match the tint of my oversize breast,
my overbalanced, exploratory tail.
                              Though I can appear
as shaky and awkward as the reversed
banner unfolding behind a propeller plane,

my confidence is real.
Beyond that I can't say just how I feel.
To catch me at rest,
you must wait all the hours of my working day and then add one.
No human being has seen my nest.
That doesn't mean I never have, or had, one.

Electrical Flora

for Elizabeth Treadwell

flowers of smoke

who put the ear
        in spirit the eye
in surprise

who obscured
        the hiding I
in annelise or analyse

we parents take care of whomever
        we used to be

who put the host
        in ghost

flowers of mist

perhaps an erasable
                kiss

not to know if we want
        oblivion

or something finer

sniff this bouquet
        then say whether

you'd rather
        be minor

flowers of osiris

and other stories in which
      dismembered daddies obviously come back
thanks to the will and recognized labors
      of mommies who never
have time to do anything else

flowers of no

to be happy
      is to be vulnerable

sadness is amour
      or armor

know who you're sad for

flowers of spring

from underneath the berm
      to open meticulous sedimentary nest

or if we change kingdoms then
      the message when the epicotyl
           arrives

I live in midair
      I greet you from there

My 1986

I painted all ten of my toenails with Liquid Paper
then followed my father's injunction and scraped it all off.

The girl I admired second-most in the world
knew how to win any argument, and how to spin,

between thumb and index finger, a ballpoint pen.
I dated her best friend for almost exactly six hours

before she broke up with me over the cordless phone,
explaining, correctly, that I had turned into her shadow.

I failed to assemble, from papier-mâché and duct tape,
a glowing, foot-long, love-potion-dispensing flower

for our production of *A Midsummer Night's Dream*.
We used a green wire. I never made props again.

That summer, I peered at the populous universe
through bangs and swaths of hair I tried to comb

and could not comb. I believed I could really fit in
with hippies, if only I met enough of them.

In my late night aerie, my upstairs writer's retreat,
I typed my ten-page poem about a dour,

shy angel confused by his runaway body.
I put an alliteration in every line

as a way to define my own verse style,
along with adapted prose from the character study

I wrote longhand in 1985,
when I felt sure that only if people unlike me—

girls, for example—would read it could the time
it took to revise it ever seem worthwhile.

Water Strider

I could look down on myself, if I let myself
reflect on my reflection endlessly,
and make a depression of every sunny day.

Instead I try hard to stay still,
to look as if I could do better than to will,

in the deaf heat of summer, this unending listening
to the hum of the scrim of beige over chlorophyll.

The longer I stay up, the more difficult
staying up gets, and the easier it looks,

as in most arts.
I view the lucid surface I inhabit
less as home than as a second skin.

Yet I have an appetite. I have mouthparts.
When I detect a dragonfly I invert
myself and break the meniscus to grab it.

On so many other ponds
stand entities much like me
though I cannot be moved to greet them as kin.

It would take more time
than you have for me to explain why I never fall in.

Gymnastics Stephanie

I am in at least two sorts of race with my body, where "with" means both "riding in and by means of" and "against, viewing it as a competitor": what can I get myself to learn to do and to do as soon as possible in the competitive moment or minute or day or month or calendar year before its changes take the willingness or the supposedly fearless patience (whatever that means) or the ability away

> practice practice practice practice look at me practice don't look at me head over
> head over heels over head over heels and practice practice

whether any of the people watching me who have not done the things I do know what I can do or what I have been trying to do or how hard it can be or how easy it seemed before I knew what I was doing not that I know what I am doing now

> practice beyond the interminable practice might be the effortless practice practice
> or apparently effortless practice or something like joy

only my peers understand me (if they do)   maybe I have no peers

to prepare for years to concentrate   for the entirety of a life

(short as it seems to adults) to see   eternity as a warm-up and a walk-through

for a minute and a half   to be and to show what you are

> over and steady two hurtles flic-flac this is what you had practiced practice practice
> practice practice practice practice practice practice practice practice practice practice

to have become someone who has to be   only what you show the world

that's what you are   so soon   it will be what you were

maybe someday I can have   a move named after me

the rotation the rounded arc the stick   that casual fans and families know

the return from infinite vertical space   into human time

what is amazing to amateurs   has to become

second nature   no marvel a stopwatch to me

     two hurtles flic-flac this is what you had practiced practice practice practice practice
     practice practice practice practice practice practice practice practice two folds more

there used to always be   a balance beam in my dreams

and the sensation of turning   over and over into the Amanar space

the pale blue and all too exciting   wish never to land

to have become someone who has to be   only what you show the world

that's what you are   so soon   it will be what you were

Cicadas

They want it to be the same thing
to be born and to turn seventeen.

See how long they waited,
how similar they are
to what they were.

Stridulation is an educational
name for their repetitive song
that does not sound, to outsiders, like music at all.

Litterbugs, shutterbugs, clicking practitioners
of non-attachment to what was their skin and their clothes—

It took such time
before they could look you in the eye,
and make an impression beyond the asynchronous
husk or mask of what they used to be.

As you sweep the rest of them off
the hood and front seat of your car, your porch, hat brim, etc.

remember why they can't help but leave
these hollow parts that were not so much *theirs*
as *them*.

We are already done. It wasn't fair.

We will bury ourselves
again, after our one
ride through your duplicitous, temperate air.

My 1987

I listened to boys I no longer wanted to know
debating the hotness of movie stars, but I
wanted nothing more than my hand in a training bra.

Once I told Annabelle, over the phone, that I loved her,
I hurtled downstairs to play Billy Joel on our spinet,
which I did, beaming or grinning, until dinnertime.

I had another life, in which I wore plate armor,
and another other life, which I preferred,
where I wore a form-fitting tunic and Mary Janes

whose contours I drew on graph paper, over and over.
In that life my chief power was reading minds;
though useful in battle, my power was tragic

on schooldays, because I had no way to turn it off.
My name was Psyche. She was melancholy,
with oversized eyelashes. She, in turn, wished she could fly.

I told myself that I would tell myself years later
that this was how I saw myself, back then.
I felt that I had become "unstuck in time,"

like baffled, wise Billy Pilgrim in *Slaughterhouse-Five*.
When I heard a trio of seniors who wore
black jeans and Dr. Martens and janitor's-key-ring chains

say they wanted a keyboard player, I put down my spoon
and sprinted across the lunchroom to tell them that I
could play the piano, and would get a keyboard soon.

School Smoking Lounge Stephanie

How many other bad habits

will I acquire while I am still
"too young to know any better," supposed

to remain obsidian, changeable, naive
(a creature of glitter, impatient for November dusk)

knowing already that sooner, rather than later,
I would do better by learning to give them all up?

Palinode with Study Guide, Spackling Knife, and Sewing Kit

Let the record—if
there is a record—show
how much of it, after a certain age, was delight:

the virgin daiquiris on New Year's Eve
and staying up till two, and other convivialities
around paintbrush, scrim, plywood, tacks, and drills
behind the scenes behind the scenes,

the hour on the telephone attempting to decode
"Ask" and "Panic" and (hardest of all) "Golden Lights"
and then the hour trying to decide
whether we spent too much time on the phone,

and the pushbutton desk-set answers for which we received
a sport's immediate rewards
that quickened us all in turn, and the sprawl
on Fridays when we occupied the whole
of the carpeted first floor hall, and the heroic
or picaresque car,
nicknamed the Green Hornet,
whose fearless owner gave us rides to school . . .

such parts of an early life
that do not require new frames—
that were almost just
fine as they were, or at least as they are.

After Callimachus

Why do I write? Experience
    and scientific evidence agree:
an otherwise intolerable load
    of shame decreases by up to six percent
if told to even a temporary companion,
    through a folded-up page at recess, a performance
on classical guitar, a palinode,
    a Tumblr, or a hash mark on a tree;
fears diminish, at least a little, whenever secrets
    are no longer secrets and enter the common
atmosphere, even as birdsong, even in code.

Sadder

Honor existing commitments,
      but don't make any new ones: that
is what my mirror image said to me,
      the one in the passenger-side
sun-visor's fold-out
      mirror that never sleeps—

If you hold to the highest standard
      everything people have made,
eventually you will love only unimproved nature,
      says the corrosive breeze; and wish-fulfillment

      is the hidden
goal of every poem,
      except when it is the obvious
goal, in which case the hidden
      goal is something like *learn*
how to live in this world. Whatever
      matters cannot be created,
says the false harbor,
      though it can be easily destroyed—

      Oh sad-hatted midday pedestrians
in nearly frozen air
      on the two-lane road before the ocean
in Barrington, where the sea-wind-
      tolerant shrubs encroach, and industry never was,
and nothing is sweet and everything is salt
      and the author of *String Light* and *ShallCross*
no longer has your back—

each grain could be the last
        in an arc whose end we know
and all the far whitecaps are rescue hounds who want
        to run as fast as they
were once rewarded for running, and will not run,
        or not with such enthusiasm, not ever again.

A Nickel on Top of a Penny

after César Vallejo

I am going to disappear in Belmont,
after taking a walk in intermittent rain.
I will vanish one day in Belmont—don't correct me—
on a warm day like today, a Thursday, in fall.

I know it even more than I know how we all want
contradictory things, like security and excitement,
immortality, hang gliders, gumdrops, a home, and all
the space in the world—Eden, Paris, Tokyo, Cockaigne.

My writing hand hurts. To the good friends who asked me to dinner,
I'm afraid I should tell you not to expect me.
When you set the table, say, "Stephanie couldn't be here,
although we were good to her; we gave her presents

for Christmas and such; we answered most of her letters,
importunate as they became; we tried not to offend her;
we sat through her chatter about piano lessons,

and telephoned her in the midst of a snowstorm last year.
We think we could not have treated her any better.
We never believed she'd simply disappear."

Advice from the Lights

If you don't get too close to people you can't disappoint them,
which would be so much worse
than letting them disappoint you.

To the extent that you gain
a perch that means other people look up to you,
to just that extent you can never
tell them how you feel.

You can warble, or
follow a siren, or a Shenandoah
vireo, into the shade, or take
advice from the lights: be
a child, or be like a child.
You will want for nothing, and you will never be heard.

Anubis

dog-jackal-god-judge

Follower-on. Latecomer. Always backward,
    a turn of the ears, of fine hairs on the ears, of the head.
A finer sense of motion. An *arrière-garde*.

    An interest in the future of the living
      as it is figured
in the unsatisfiable
    demands of the dead.

         •

My chambers are lit from within, or else
from above, like
         embers, unilaterally.

I study what you call spontaneity.

The life in which I can learn,
albeit after the fact, what all of you
have done with yourselves—going nowhere, seeing
every piquant possibility—

turned out to be
the only life for me.

         •

Dog lovers, I have learned, have feline souls, requiring
    companionship they cannot "find within,"

whereas the poor souls and pilgrims who look up to cats
admire their independence and amorality,

we ourselves being already
"guilty as sin."

•

I watch the gate.
Why do you not go through?
Then there would be no one to watch the gate.

•

Where would you place yourself?
I cannot say,
given the obvious conflicts of interest;
as long as I stay

at my post, without respite or rest,
nobody else can either. Not knowing is best.

Paper Stephanie

I am less flimsy than boys think.
I can stand up with some help. I can raise my hand,
my glass or my bangle or my japonaiserie fan,
though never all four at once. I know
the name of the artist who made me and made my hair,
with its scribbles and angles, and my other hair,
with its Byzantine curves and its coils, and my other hair,
that I wore when I was a flapper. I have been cut out,
refolded, unfolded, and put back into a folder;
I have been lost and found and lost and found.

Someday I will be left in a cardboard box,
the kind loosely associated with shoes.
Should I fear scissors, or love them? Once
I was colorless, I was self-consciously artistic,
I was a fluster magnet, I was scared.
I rang my new telephone. I was the belle of a ball
where even the gloves were bell-shaped. I could not hear.
I did not look like me at all.

A pencil mark grazes my ankle. A chestnut
stallion, tilted an inch off the vertical,
propped on three out of four legs, watches over me
from the jury-rigged off-white lean-to of an envelope
that serves him as a bedroom or a stall.

What if I had a side you could not see?
Once I was interchangeable, then I was loved,
and now I am not so sure. I have been upside down,
my face in thick carpet, in coach and spring-wheeled trap,
my ballet shoes, riding boots, and brickle-edge tap
shoes circled around me. None of it hurt.
I fear misadventure, and yet I would like to be shown.
I fray and sag in my thick bustle, my tan riding skirt,
my mythical petticoats. Maybe I'll never leave home.

Helium

Inhale enough and you too
can get light-headed, momentarily
forget yourself, as with nitrous, or choking, or sex,
which can also make people squeak.

Mineralogists say we are taking it
out of the Earth at an unsustainable pace,
forgoing industrial safety and physics experiments
in order to throw better birthday parties and make
acquaintances' voices temporarily high.

Untold amounts are made
each day inside the unattainable stars,
which thereby grow denser, and that much closer to ending.
We cannot make it here, though some of us try.

I know of a child so sensitive, so used
to having whatever would sadden or weigh her down,
kept out of her life, that when she came to learn
about the expansion of the universe,
its redshift like a great balloon
with no skin, no pop, just the fact of everything
growing, over time, ever farther apart,
she would drink only water, and took to her bed for a week.

A Crime at Pattaya

The following year, in a highly publicized case, four transvestites (one a trans-
sexual) robbed a Hong Kong businessman and others by first inducing their
victims to suck on their nipples, which had been coated with a tranquilizer.
                            —Holly Brubach, *Girlfriend: Men, Women, and Drag*

I would do it again. I felt
paradoxically adult—
each chevron on each wave on that warm ocean
pointing backwards and up the pale twist
in the shadow below concrete stairs. I was led by my wrist.
There was a great oval mirror,
the hush of a closing door,
two earrings unhooked and a square plastic bottle of lotion.

There was a bare smooth shoulder, and suppler hands
than mine on the buttons around my collar and neck,
my clavicle, my sternum, and points just south.
There was an oversized rocking chair, and a rock
that shone like a wet star-opal around her throat,
her fuschia lips, her softer mouth,
and commands that could never have felt like commands.
She was a moonless night at the prow of a boat,
and I was a pilot, a ghost in the womb: I obeyed.

I woke up to mopeds, car horns, and particulate haze.
I had wet myself. I had slept for two days.
The consul had come and gone, leaving ill-fitting shoes,
but I walked away shaking and barefoot. I would have paid,
and happily, twice as much as I lost, to lose
my reason again so utterly: how could I choose
to leave this beach forever, this tideless fold
with its plain rice and its thin shade,
where for the first time I lost it all, got rolled,
erased, knocked out, taken for granted, and was not afraid?

The Sun Rising

awake awake
diminishing
shade on sheets

sends lovers to their
bailiwicks & children
to their parents' haunts & turns

so many adults
from when
will you love me to when

will you love me again
maturity
means a bed that is

the reverse or revenge
of the princess
& the pea

when you dream
I don't know what you see
in me

Royal Botanical

Edinburgh

From the top you can see the whole city, as if on a plate.

·

The big Chinese flora that are not quite hibiscus,
the pale striated blue of ghosts or gowns.

·

The wild gargantuan hosta
like the one that took over our garden,
big enough to hide
a kitten or a child.

·

A Japanese maple hunched over in full bloom
like an adult bending down to a first grader—
no, like Snuffleupagus,
all his shade still inside him,
now visible when cameras catch him, or when the sun shines,

above the oversized, gangly, overlapping
stalks of the yellow giant iris,
whose feathery inflorations are definitely—
no, definitely not—
the hue of Big Bird.

·

The daisy, or day's-eye. The black-eyed Susan. The egg
and whatever might hatch from that egg,
and whatever parent or teacher can tend
the egg, since hiding it is, by now, out of the question.

•

Eternal return: the scruff or fluff
across the back of the bumblebee
who picks and nudges her way across red clover,

whose wings like pedals and wheels
mean nothing is ever over.
Having been fourteen

for 25 years, I agree, and cannot tell
if it is a fact through which,
like the vascular stems, I draw strength,
or a truth from which I may never recover.

•

Plant better local flowers for the bees,
lest the rest of them get up and leave.

Dear travelers, dear
gardeners: do not ask us to go back
to an order in which you no longer believe.

Pastorale

The beloved wool skirt, the beaten-down hooded sweatshirt
with its stamped-in unpronounceable band name,
the tasseled vintage spring-weight brand-name
cardigan with its ever-
wider lavender stripes, and other
woven things inertia tends to pull apart—
for such objects, it's work
not only to stay together, but not to look hurt,
to appear, though worse for wear, never-
theless worn out of loyalty and love,
so that we take, from the loosening fabric, what memory will give,
possessions we already trust,
ways to recognize one another in wintry weather,
and not (the sheer patch of silver
on the checkerboard scarf admits) that we were just cold,
that we dressed in a rush, that we are just
like shepherds with one sheepfold,
who have one cloak, and no alternative.

Advice or Prayer for Airports

There are no lords

We should protect one another

Let the technology work
until it fails

Until it is free
to rust

Let each pixel and tap
on the shoulder show
us where we cannot stay

Where someone else
needs the fee

Let us be like
the insects that ride
in droplets

From one habitat to another

Bromeliad dwellers

Trumpet

Resilient tears

Indian Stream Republic

No one should be this alone—
none of the pines
in their prepotent verticals,

none of the unseen
hunters or blundering moose
who might stop by the empty lodge or the lake

as blue as if there had never been people
although there are people: a few
at the general store, and evidence of more

in clean vinyl siding, and down the extended street
a ruddy steel pole the height of a child, its plaque
remembering a place called *Liberty*

at Indian Stream, 1832–35,
between the disputed boundaries
of Canada and New Hampshire, meant

as temporary, almost
content to remain its own.
Each household, their constitution said, could possess

one cow, one hog, one gun,
books, bedding and hay, seven sheep and their wool, secure
from attachment for debt no matter the cause.

The state militia came to set them right.
The legerdemain of the noon sun through needles and leaves,
revealing almost nothing, falls across

thin shadows, thin trace of American wheels and hands
for such high soil and such short reward:
the people . . . do hereby mutually agree

to form themselves into a body politic
by the name of Indian Stream, and in that capacity
to exercise all the powers of a sovereign

till such time as we can ascertain to what
government we properly belong.

Écossaise

As you took a green apple and rubbed its round form clean
in the black cotton of your practical, scoop-neck top
so that part of the apple could almost
settle, or seem to settle, between your breasts,

seat 71B, British Airways 215,

the scent of your red-gold hair unaccountably
a bit like rose, a bit like rosemary
in the polymer-plastic new-car atmosphere of the plane,

I thought of the painting we saw on our last day there
of the Reverend Robert Walker, the delighted
minister of the Canongate Kirk
on ice skates, his tiny red laces
perpendicular to each other,
of the off-center, overturned Y that his tilted
body, hat, coat, and leggings made, black on black
on black on black on black, then rose on black,
and of the receding, or reticent, gray of the lake,

the innocence of his pleasure, his one-legged pose.

Spoken for a Pair of Ferrets

Too serious
no longer, we
        have learned to love
        our restlessness
whose tussles left
us short of breath.
        We wrestled with
        the reckless flesh
that both of us
would test & test
        then half refresh
        & half forget
to use what's left
in each of us:
        vitality
        we live to spend—
to roll, unroll
& revel in
        our toothed excess
        of wildness—
would in the wild
be what it took
        to nose fresh eggs
        past lips of nests
or drag mole rats
from burrows. Where
        we live determines
        what we do,
how frivolous
or violent
        we have to be.
        Captivity

thus keeps us fresh.
Our arguments
        are circular:
        we love to writhe,
to form a wreath
or flare & tie
        ourselves in knots
        like ropewalks' nets.
Come play with us,
we say, except
        you can't: wrong head
        & body shape,
wrong tibias
& scapulas.
        If we invite
        you anyway,
it's just to tease
you for your lack
        of torque, your
        inabilities.
Refusing the
imperative
        to work hard or
        make more of us,
our nature is
evading nature's laws,
        all over each
        other or always on
each other's
backs, with half-
        retracted claws.

After Callimachus

It's hard work making people fall in love,
        even harder to get them to stay that way. No wonder
my friend Simone has built, for the goddess of love,
        an idiosyncratic altar:
on it, one tube of lip gloss, a charm bracelet, car keys,
        a rental agreement for a basement apartment,
a doorbell, a star for a Christmas tree, a salt or
        pepper shaker, the mouthpiece
for a half-size trumpet, a pill splitter, and under
        them all, a folded velvet satchel,
                in which the lucky couple
        who stay together into a shared old age
can keep whatever other sentiment-
        al objects they decide to save.

Tiara Stephanie

If the root
of experience is humiliation,

a wound that the world (without sorcery) cannot make good,

what does the root do to hide itself from the full tree?

What is the root of mystery?

What is the difference
between a cry of pain
and a cry of pain,

and how do I pick up
enough sense to come out of the rain?

I shall stand in it this afternoon, letting my cotton T-shirt soak through,

right into my shorts, right down my new white tights
and the rain boots beneath them, like last-minute help,

delighted not to be dissolving, not to be made

of sugar and flour, keeping the dirt off my cheeks,

thinking "This has to be a dream,

I do not know whether I want it to be a dream,

whether I want it to have been a dream."

Secondhand Flashlight

I have no say
over who or what turns me on,
only the power to make things clear as day,

or, at least, as a truculent dawn.
Once a girl brought me to a rave;
I was dizzy, then giddy, then woke up near dead on a lawn.

When I look back to my origins, I crave
that chastity, that darkness, but not yet.
I also scare skunks off and represent ways to look brave.

I can render the same silhouette
gargantuan or gaunt,
or shake and make it dance a minuet;

it's you who choose what I appear to flaunt.
When all the people around me are fully aware
of whatever's in front

of their faces, where all their acquaintances are
and how to find loose change they think they lost,
I sleep in my drawer;

I prove I am worth the $1.50 I cost
when the power goes out, and at parties with nothing else
that can distract a preschool guest

or coax shy grownups from their shells.
I might be the first thing a kid ever put together.
I do just what my battery compels.

Unlike my big brother
the limelight and my cousin the campfire, I prefer inconsequence:
though famous in culverts and attics, I would rather

play no role in public events.
I have never—can never—run wild.
Obtuse, hollow-bodied, confined to the present tense,

I'll be your lightsaber if you are a child,
though first and last I do no harm.
In bad dreams I see miles

of anthracite burn; in my best I keep somebody warm.
Sunlight to me is just something I get shut off in.
Having resigned myself to my fixed form,

I was surprised to escape the cardboard coffin
of the charity shop that sold me.
Though none of my parts can soften,

the humid summer air can still corrode me.
Pick me up; test me every so often. Hold me.

Creative Writing

The sea on its shore, for example,
            especially near high tide,
and the plain green pennants by the lifeguards'
            scantily painted wooden chairs, poles posted
in pairs, like rhymes. SWIM BETWEEN FLAGS.
            It's a safety thing
            and therefore easily disregarded,
like the fox heads, tiger swallowtail
            wings, horses' teeth, antennae and paws
in the clouds that convene or loom just below the far fence,
            the fence that keeps the dunes
from spilling and falling apart all over the gentler
            roads and beach-roses
            below the actual beach. It is as if
they had something to learn, but something that no
            human being can teach:
            about limits, about the end
of everything visible, maybe, or about
            the makeup of imaginary air.
            Meanwhile there
            are the distant preteen waders,
            the scribble and froth of shallows,
the competition or hidden cooperation
            recorded in the tracks of hungry gulls,
            where everything
            means something, but never for long,
and the clouds and the absence of clouds are both
            clichés, like countable sheep
            about to be shorn,
            or only temporarily forlorn.

Final Exam Stephanie

Please turn in or leave behind any scratch materials. You have now agreed
to follow all the rules. Good girls will be notified sooner. Next year you are
going. You have to look forward to until.

Like walking out of an uncompleted pencil sketch, an unprimed canvas, the
torn-off end of a page, like being a bracket in the fragment of ancient Greek
that I encountered in my best friend's photograph. Nobody

is going to report me if I break down, break up, break in three, like a bone left
to us from beach week's campfire feast

> like the page after the last
> page of a comic book
>
> like whatever takes place under the oblong
> gleam on microscope glass
>
> like the white space between the grays
> of a birch branch shadow on snow
>
> like the aluminum ladder in our basement
> on its side on the cold concrete going nowhere

It's June. I have a new and golden pendant, a folding hand mirror, a calculator
too. Its heft in my hand grins like a mirror pointed back at the sun.

What is this air, this space in which nobody rewards

me for conformity,

or punishes me, or keeps

track of my time, what I wear, how I see

myself, or tries to tell me what my name should be?

Advice for Holding Together

Here is a shoelace
tougher than snakeskin
coarser than coats' wool

Under each spiral
a union of polymers
structurally analogous

To the transatlantic cable

To the supposed
progress of civilization

To anything else you can worry
between thumb and ring

Held together so that it
can work at all
by the aglet at each end

What you can't hear
may be deafening somebody else

What's almost too small
to see may just be far away

Be your own means
of magnification or microscopy

Become your own
indignity

Tourmalines

I used to collect them;
they gather a charge under pressure, piezoelectric
(I was proud to know the word),
semiprecious when clear, pink or green; mine were half an inch thick,
striated, unpopular, cheap enough to hoard.
In science museums and gift shops I learned to detect them
amid the stacks of greater souvenirs.

At the Smithsonian's cavernous
Museum of Natural History, for example,
on the first floor, to the right, in the minerals hall
behind the apparently ravenous
wooden *T. rex*, I could pick out a thumb-sized sample
for the price of a Superball,
then wait in the rotunda with my peers,
sixth-grade boys and girls in puffy coats.

The girls put their hair up as if for a special occasion;
the boys slouched, weedy, scared.
The taxidermy elephant seemed to frown.
A few blocks down, the Democrats under Reagan
were trading away their votes;
they filed like visitors into the Senate, prepared
to watch the Great Society come down.

Washingtonian

Snap and crackle of pairs of squirrels—gray-black and pale
in the middens of dying leaves before the ravine
that separate North Portal from Portal Street

is like the crackle and pop of the breakfast cereal
that dazzled a generation on TV,
though it was nothing special on the spoon;

and the news that a TV appearance
by your favorite spangled pop star was lip-synched
may vary in its importance or disappointment

depending on whether there is independent
evidence she can carry a tune.
As for the discontent in the silhouettes

of larches and beeches, trees that treat their lawns
as audiences for the prosperity
of those who lived there or live there today—

ask them what joy would replace
the joys they appear to erase.
Ask them how to imagine pulling up roots
where they have, or could have had, a chance to stay.

Advice from Rock Creek Park

What will survive us
has already begun

Oak galls
Two termites' curious
self-perpetuating bodies

Letting the light through the gaps

They lay out their allegiances
under the roots
of an overturned tree

Almost always better
to build than to wreck

You can build in a wreck

Under the roots
of an overturned tree

Consider the martin that hefts
herself over traffic cones

Consider her shadow
misaligned
over parking-lot cement
Saran Wrap scrap in her beak

Nothing lasts
forever not even
the future we want

The president has never
owned the rain

Suspense

A way of holding things up, as the Zakim Bridge
holds up the cables that hold up
the nearly horizontal wedge and grids
that hold the boxed-in traffic in its variable
progress north to Somerville.

It holds us taut. It stretches out our days.
Without its gates and levels, we would slip
too rapidly off and onward, towards the end
which is the only end
no storyteller knows, or disobeys.

December 2016

Sea ponders and then
pillages the land

•

Tonight the supermoon
no bigger than a regular full moon really
but brighter
almost terrifying
not to be looked at directly
a lidless eye

•

I used to think
that all of us followed the furrows
of the same plow

but then the rains
and then no rain

the millipedes scuffle and scuttle in
the fading gutter-pan and tire track

the reaped field is an altar
overturned

•

Two magenta—no, two hot pink child-sized gloves
abandoned in a host of fallen leaves
by a chain-link fence

What is natural

•

Indoors the pet cat rummaging
making the laundry pile his ship's
galley his miniature ocean
knows something he does not know he knows

the fate of civilizations
fresh sandbox sand in the dewclaw
coastal erosion
or where the time goes

•

There is no machine
nothing works
it's the scene in *Disgrace*
where David decides to put the animal down

not because "his time
has come" but because everyone's
time comes and no one else will feed him now

•

There is no rule of law
except for what you imagine
which other people may then proceed to ignore

So say a tight-lipped prayer
to the goddess of second chances
wherever she renews her tasks

Civilization's a split wind a confidence game
put your lips next to a dead leaf and blow it away

while saying you hope
it will be there the following day

Resolved

Not to come
between grain and gleaners
a child and another child

Bring your mite to the dusk

Do better than the best of all possible
government
in the worst of all likely worlds

Consider the sun as it rises
only
slightly over the moon's lip

turning the lifeless craters
from rose
to rose-gold

not caring
where
or whether
anything grows

No one has
to be told

Fuzzy Golem Doll with 6" Keychain

Altneu Synagogue, Prague

Protector of children from boredom, of parents from fear
of not bringing anything halfway appropriate back,
I want to be chosen. I have seen,
week after week, cliques of visitors check
my price tag. I keep trying to count them. I keep losing track.

My grandfather and namesake lived for truth
or a word that meant truth,
and was killed by the word for death, and brought to life
by a collective wish for a dispassionate
lowbrow hero with feet of clay.
Whatever made him famous he did with his hands.
He may or may not have been able
to do a good deed,
to interpret, as well as follow, simple commands.

Once I belong to you, you can take me downstairs.
A queue of high stains on the wainscot serves to remember
the existential threat of 2002,
when the Quarter flooded, and the water entered.
Each wooden seat bears a brass nameplate. In the one center
of the sunken, holy, rectilinear area,
a cast-iron cage awaits cantillation and prayer.

What you inherit depends
not least on what you can make.
In my own recessed and featureless
interior I hold,
along with a spell or scroll
for strength, a rabbinical saying:

Carry these two truths in your back pocket
and take them out as occasion demands:
on the one side, I am dust and ashes,
on the other, The world was created for my sake.

Concord Grapes

What would it be like to belong
entirely in your own body, or in your own country, or at
your own address? It might
be like these unselfconscious, tangled, each-
one-over-the-next-one Concord grapes,
hooked (as in hook-and-eye) on the chain-link fence
between our driveway and the next;
the populous dewy clusters
hang as if lashed
to so many miniscule masts,
or threaded and caught in the stems of their earnest
commensals and competitors.
Each skin gives its possessor neither shelter
nor camouflage, only a violet luster
that catches the eye. For such a wild
varietal to thrive,
let alone spread, it has to be
consumed. The state seal
of Connecticut, designed
in 1639, depicts
three poles, each supporting a hefty cluster
of purplish discs, over Latin
that means "Who transplants,
sustains." On each, a serpentine
red line—a thickening vine,
though elsewhere it could read
as a caduceus, or a dollar sign—
connects the grapes it does not quite entwine.
When the first Europeans to try Concord grapes
made wine,
they found it repellently sweet—
as if a less-than-competent
goblin or vintner had meant

to intoxicate children. So they drank
their barrel ciders and mashed these into jam.
Two hundred years later, Ralph Waldo Emerson thanked
"embattled farmers" for firing the grape-
sized "shot heard round
the world"; not many years
or compromises afterward, Julia Ward Howe
predicted the "trampling out"
of "vintage," if not the scavenger-mutilated
or putrefying corpses of Shiloh
and Andersonville, who "died
to make men free." Unpicked, the grapes
have a musky, or dusky, hue, especially
at dusk, although their promise of easy
separation from the stem is not
to be trusted; fingered, they often fall off
and into the thicket they made, as if
once ripe, they would rather wither
than give
pleasure to us, who have
taken more than our share. The English Romantics preferred,
when they were moved to speak of revolution,
a series of metaphors about dawn.
The motion-sensor-operated
lights that hang, and sometimes swing,
like tennis rackets, from the corners
of our eaves over the fence are always darkest
just before they get turned on.

White Lobelia

Little megaphones,
we hang out in the garden center and gossip
with the petunias three seasons a year.

With leaves too small to resemble
thumbs or hands or hearts, too soft
for any parts
of our threadable stems to grow thorns,
we prefer to pretend we are horns,
cornets and alto sax, prepared to assemble
in studios and sight-read any charts.

We are, of course, for sale
to generous homes. Some of us have become
almost overfamiliar with ornamental
cabbage, with the ins and outs of kale.
Others have lost our voice
in a painstaking effort to justify our existence
as a perennial second choice.

Like you, we dismiss whatever comes easiest
to us and overestimate what looks hard.
In our case that means we admire
our neighbors' luxuriant spontaneities
and treat the most patient preparers with disregard.

We strive for contentment in our
hanging baskets once
we know we will not touch ground.
We tell ourselves
and one another that if you listen
with sufficient
generosity, you will be able
to hear our distinctive and natural sound.

Notes

In poems that appear to hold details from my own life, many names and details have been changed, some real events combined, and some events invented. Putt-Putt Mini Golf, however, was a real miniature golf course and video arcade in Montgomery County, Maryland. The first three lines in part 2 of "Cloud Studies" adapt remarks by Jordan Ellenberg. Several people will recognize details from "Palinode with Study Guide, Spackling Knife, and Sewing Kit"; I am particularly grateful to Eric Meyer and to Sally Grant.

All the poems titled "After Callimachus" grow out of poems by the ancient Greek Alexandrian poet Callimachus. "So reactionaries . . ." grows out of the prologue to the *Aetia* (sometimes called "Against the Telchines"); "Half of me . . ." out of epigram 42; "It's hard work . . . ," out of epigram 34.

For more on Scott Miller, Game Theory, and the Loud Family, the musical subjects of "Over Sacramento," please see www.loudfamily.com. Many of their records are again available on streaming media and as CD reissues from Omnivore Records; you can read Miller's own critical writings in his collection *Music: What Happened?*

In "Esprit Stephanie," Esprit, or ESPRIT, was and is a line of clothing popular in the 1980s, known for its stencil-like logo, and still available today.

"Mean Girls" incorporates imitations of Charles Baudelaire's (much shorter) "Femmes damnées." "A Nickel on Top of a Penny" incorporates imitations of César Vallejo's "Piedra negra sobre una piedra blanca."

Details in "Indian Stream Republic" come from Daniel Doan's study *Indian Stream Republic: Settling a New England Frontier* (Hanover: UPNE, 1997) and from the present-day town of Pittsburg, New Hampshire.

In "December 2016," *Disgrace* is the novel by J. M. Coetzee.

In "Fuzzy Golem Doll with 6" Keychain," "Keep two truths in your pocket . . ." appears in the American Reform Jewish prayer book for High Holidays (Rosh Hashanah and Yom Kippur), where it is labeled only "Chasidic, 18th century"; Martin Buber, in *Tales of the Hasidim*, attributes it to Rabbi Simcha Bunim (or Bunem or Bunam). "The world was created for my sake": Mishnah Sanhedrin 4:5; "dust and ashes": Genesis 18:27.

"Concord Grapes" draws on Sarah Oktay, "Native Divine Vine: Nantucket's Fox Grape," *Yesterday's Island* 38:3 (May 2008), readable as of early 2017 at http://www.yesterdaysisland.com/2008/features/foxgrape.php.

Acknowledgments

Many poems in this book have appeared in journals, on websites, or in anthologies (sometimes in earlier versions, or with different titles). I am grateful to them, to their staff members, and to their editors:

The Account, The Academy of American Poets Poem-a-Day, The American Scholar, The Ampersand Review, Aspasiology, The Awl, The Believer, Blackbox Manifold, Blue Earth Review, Boston Review, Copper Nickel, EOAGH, Five Points, Free Verse, The Globe and Mail (Canada), *The Iowa Review, The Hampden-Sydney Poetry Review, HiLobrow, John Donne and Contemporary Poetry* (Palgrave, 2017), *Lady Churchill's Rosebud Wristlet, Lit Hub, Locomotive* (Armenia), *London Review of Books, Luna Luna, Michigan Quarterly Review, Nat Brut, The New Republic, The New Yorker, The Ocean State Review, The Paris Review, Partisan, PN Review, Poems for Political Disaster* (Boston Review, 2017), *Poetry, Prac Crit, Prelude, Provincetown Arts Journal, Sport* (New Zealand), *T: The New York Times Style Magazine, Vetch: A Magazine of Trans Poetry and Poetics, The Virginia Quarterly Review, The Washington Post, The Wolf.*

Thanks of a special order go to Marisa Atkinson, Katie Dublinski, Fiona McCrae, Jeff Shotts, and everyone else at Graywolf Press; to my colleagues at Harvard University and at the University of Canterbury in Christchurch and in particular to the relevant chairs at those institutions, James Engell, James Simpson, and Paul Millar; to Blue Flower Arts; to *Boston Review* editors and staff; and to the Guggenheim Foundation.

Poems with "Stephanie" as part of the title, as well as the poem "Mean Girls," were previously published in the chapbook *All-Season Stephanie* (Minneapolis: Rain Taxi Editions, 2015), which also includes illustrations by Eowyn Evans and poems not collected here. Special thanks to Kelly Everding and Eric Lorberer.

For other help, advice, encouragement and assistance—emotional, literary and practical—directly reflected within poems and in the ordering of this book,

I am deeply grateful to: Sandra Beasley, Alfred Bendixen, Susan Bianconi, David Blair, Lucie Brock-Broido, Sandra and Jeffrey Burt, David Caplan, Timothy Donnelly, Mark Doten, Jordan Ellenberg, Jonathan Ellis, Josh Glenn, Rachel Gold, Jorie Graham, Langdon Hammer, Laura Kasischke, J. D. McClatchy, Matt McGowan, the Nelson Patel family, Mark Payne, Trace Peterson, Chris Price, Justin Quinn, Dean Rader, Donald Revell, Michael Scharf, Michael Schmidt, Don Share, Carmen Giménez Smith, Amber Tamblyn, Craig Morgan Teicher, Helen Vendler, Mark Wunderlich, Jane Yeh, and Monica Youn, as well as to my students, and to the dedicatees of individual poems.

And to Jessica Bennett, our Nathan and our Cooper, every day, in ways beyond all counting.

Stephen—also Steph and Stephanie—Burt is Professor of English at Harvard University and the author of several books of poetry and literary criticism, among them *Belmont*, *Parallel Play*, *Close Calls with Nonsense*, *The Forms of Youth: 20th Century Poetry and Adolescence*, and *The Poem Is You: 60 Contemporary American Poems and How to Read Them*. They grew up in and around Washington, DC, have lived in Connecticut, New York, England, New Zealand, and Minnesota, and now reside in Belmont, Massachusetts, with their spouse, Jessie, and their children, Cooper and Nathan.

The text of *Advice from the Lights* is set in Adobe Garamond Pro.
Book design by Rachel Holscher. Composition by Bookmobile Design
and Digital Publisher Services, Minneapolis, Minnesota.
Manufactured by Versa Press on acid-free, 30 percent postconsumer wastepaper.